Quality Assurance
for
Activity Programs
Second Edition

Richelle N. Cunninghis, EdM, OTR/C
Elizabeth Best-Martini, MS, CTRS, ACC

Published and distributed by

Idyll Arbor, Inc.

PO Box 720, Ravensdale, WA 98051 (206) 432-3231

Editor: joan burlingame, CTRS, HTR
Cover photograph "Between a Rock and a Hard Place" by Thomas
M. Blaschko.

Table of Contents

Publisher's Note:

The term "activity professional" is used throughout this book. By "activity professional" we mean an individual who provides activity services to residents in long term care settings including those who are (but, of course not limited to):

- Activity Assistant, Certified
- Activity Consultant, Certified
- Activity Director, Certified
- Art Therapist
- Dance Therapist
- Horticultural Therapist, Registered
- Music Therapist, Registered
- Occupational Therapist, Registered
- Occupational Therapy Assistant, Certified
- Recreational Therapist, NCTRC Certified
- Social Worker

This book is also intended for students who are preparing to be activity professionals.

Chapter 1

Introduction

Ever since we started providing health care to others, we have been interested in improving the results. The process has become more formalized over time. Today it is called by various names including *quality assurance, quality improvement, total quality improvement* and *improving organizational performance.* When the process works well, it helps you identify how good your work is without making your work harder.

Today, quality assurance is the process of identifying problems, determining the worst problem, figuring out how to fix it and making sure that the problem does not return. To work as an activity professional today you need to know how to set up a quality assurance program, how to identify problems, how to correct them and how to monitor your progress.

You may ask, "Why do I need to create more paper work when I know what is wrong?" The answer is because the law says so and because managed care companies want to be sure that they are getting the most for their money. These days knowledge of quality assurance techniques is just as important as knowledge of the disease process, physiology, anatomy and the therapeutic process itself.

One federal law that requires quality assurance is the Omnibus Budget Reconciliation Act of 1990 or "OBRA." It requires that facilities know how well they are meeting the needs of their residents. Facilities must have a quality assurance program in place, along with a committee to identify areas that needed improvement. The law also requires a facility to design ways to improve the delivery of services and to follow-through with the changes. While the law allows the activity professional to be one of the committee members, up to now they were seldom chosen.

On July 1, 1995, the OBRA regulations were updated. There were many changes made to the original interpretation but the most significant changes were in the survey process and how the regulations are enforced. One change made it easier to identify the severity of violations. (A violation occurs when a service or piece of equipment is below standards and, therefore, potentially harmful to the resident.) The authors of the newly changed regulations realized that not all violations were an equal threat to the resident's health. To help staff make decisions about which problems to address first and to help surveyors provide consistent surveys from one facility to the next, a "grid" was developed. This grid helps identify an incident's severity and scope. (Scope looks at how often it occurred and how many people it affected.)

The grid also includes the penalties that may be applied by the survey team to assure "Substantial Compliance." (Substantial compliance is the term used to indicate that a facility is meeting the minimum expectations for providing quality services.)

A facility is expected to provide services that meet each resident's physical, social, emotional and psychological needs. However, in reality, errors happen, residents' needs are missed or not addressed, staff call in sick and other problems arise. Even the best facility has difficulty providing quality services all of the time. Because of this, each facility must have an ongoing program to identify problems, determine needed changes, make those changes and monitor the results. For such a system to work, everyone must be involved at some level.

The basic idea behind a good quality assurance program is that each department is always evaluating its services and determining areas of possible weakness. The program involves all staff members and holds each of them responsible for follow-through. This constant review is referred to as a *Continuous Quality Improvement* or *Total Quality Improvement*.

The activity professional is responsible for paying attention to his/her activity program, running his/her department and understanding the specific federal and state requirements that apply to both. For facilities that voluntarily agree to follow standards outlined by the Joint Commission for the Accreditation of Healthcare Organizations (JCAHO) or the Commission for the Accreditation of Rehabilitation Facilities (CARF), the activity professional must also meet the additional requirements of those organizations.

Even the best run department will have at least one area of service that could be improved. Under quality assurance requirements, the activity professional must identify the *most* pressing problem, have a plan to correct the problem and have documentation that progress was checked at least once every quarter. If the problem is not being corrected fast enough, the activity professional must modify the plan.

Some departments may find that they have more then one problem that is significant enough to have them out of substantial compliance (or to "fail survey"). An example is having late quarterly updates *and* having staff who forget to wash their hands between sessions (infection control). In this case, the activity professional will be tracking the progress of two plans of continuous quality improvement.

The rest of this book will help you understand the terms used when talking about quality assurance; outline the basic, minimum actions you must take to meet standards; and provide you with some of the basic policies, procedures and forms you will need to implement a continuous quality improvement program. While many of the examples in this book are from long term care settings, the information can be used in any health care setting: pediatrics, rehabilitation, psychiatry, home health care, etc.

Chapter 2

Quality Assurance

To many, it must seem that quality assurance appeared on the scene suddenly. And although everyone seems to be talking about it and many hours of staff time are taken up by it, not everyone agrees on what it is and how it is done.

As is the case with other frequently used terms, quality assurance seems to mean different things to different people. (It is even called by different names including *continuous quality improvement* and *improving organizational performance*.) In health care it is considered to be a method of evaluating services by comparing them to accepted standards. For the activity professional in long-term care, it is seen as a means to:

- monitor and evaluate the appropriateness of services provided to ensure quality of care including quality of life.
- improve that care by correcting identified problems.

There are two primary reasons we need to have quality assurance programs. First, quality assurance programs help us improve the positive impact of the services that we provide. Such programs help us measure the benefits of the care that we are currently providing. They also help us identify areas that may need to be improved. By looking at our strengths and weaknesses, we use our problem solving skills and our creative skills to improve services. Quality assurance programs should be considered "decision making tools concerned with not only what *is* but what *should be* and achieving change within a particular care setting." They should be "ongoing, objective and improvement oriented."[1]

Second, quality assurance programs are considered to be a necessary part of a good practice. Our professional organizations and the health care industry have stated that having a quality assurance program is expected. Not having one means that the professional is failing to meet standards. (No matter how good his/her practice may be!)

Legislative Requirements

The changing face of health care made accountability through the use of quality assurance programs an inevitable part of every professional's job. The requirements came from all directions: from accreditation agencies such as the Joint Commission and CARF, from the insurance companies and health maintenance organizations, from the professional organizations that represent the various professional groups and from the federal government itself. In October 1990, federal legislation required that all facilities maintain a quality assessment and assurance committee and develop a quality assurance plan to be used throughout the facility. Specific criterion was set up against which "the appropriateness, quality and necessity of health care provided by the individual department or service may be compared."[2]

The legal requirement that each department have a quality assurance program was strengthened when OBRA was updated in 1995. Now, any facility that does not have a quality assurance program for each department may be considered to be out of substantial compliance.

In order to understand the federal law requiring a quality assurance program, you must be familiar with the terminology associated with these changes.

Terminology

Deficiency: A "deficiency" is any service or equipment provided by the facility that does not meet the standards outlined in the law (regulations).

Participation: The federal government uses the term "participation" to mean that a facility is allowed to be part of the group of facilities that can obtain funding from the federal and state government because the facility has met all of the minimum requirements outlined in the law.

Substantial Compliance: A term used to mean that a facility has provided reasonable care to the residents. The OBRA law defines substantial compliance as "a level of compliance with the requirements of participation such that any identified deficiencies pose no greater risk to resident health or safety than the potential for causing minimal harm. Substantial compliance constitutes compliance with participation requirements."[3]

Severity: The federal government created four categories to reflect the level of harm as a result of inadequate care. See the chart on the next page.

Definitions of Severity[4]

Level 1 No Actual Harm with Potential for Minimal Harm	A deficiency that has the potential for causing no more than a minor negative impact on the resident(s).
Level 2 No Actual Harm with Potential for More than Minimal Harm that is not Immediate Jeopardy	Non-compliance that results in minimal physical, mental *and/or* psychosocial discomfort to the resident *and/or* has the potential (not yet realized) to compromise the resident's ability to maintain *and/or* reach his/her highest practicable physical, mental *and/or* psychosocial well being as defined by an accurate and comprehensive resident assessment, plan of care and provision of services.
Level 3 Actual Harm that is Not Immediate Jeopardy	Non-compliance that results in a negative outcome that has compromised the resident's ability to maintain *and/or* reach his/her highest practicable physical, mental *and/or* psychosocial well being as defined by the accurate and comprehensive resident assessment, plan of care and provision of services. This does not include a deficient practice that only has limited consequences for the resident and would be included in Level 2 or Level 1.
Level 4 Immediate Jeopardy	A situation in which immediate corrective action is necessary because the provider's noncompliance with one or more requirements of participation has caused, or is likely to cause, serious injury, serious harm, impairment, or death to a resident receiving care in a facility. Facility practice establishes a reasonable degree of predictability of similar actions, situations, practices, or incidents occurring in the future.

Scope: The federal government developed three categories that reflect the spread of an identified problem as shown below.

Definitions of Scope[5]

Scope	Description
Isolated	One or a very limited number of residents are affected *and/or* one or a very limited number of staff are involved *and/or* the situation has occurred only occasionally or in a very limited number of locations.
Pattern	More than a very limited number of residents are affected *and/or* more than a very limited number of staff are involved *and/or* the situation has occurred in several locations. The effect of the deficient practice is not found to be pervasive throughout the facility.
Widespread	Problems causing the deficiencies are pervasive in the facility or represent systemic failure.

Substandard Quality of Care: An official term used by the government that means that a facility did not provide reasonable care. If deficiencies are found during a survey in 483.13: Resident Behavior and Facility Practices, 483.15: Quality of Life or 483.25: Quality of Care, the survey team looks at the severity and scope of the deficiencies to determine if they represent substandard quality of care. Substandard quality of care occurs if there is immediate jeopardy to resident health or safety (level 4 severity) in any scope or if the severity is level 2 (potential for more than minimal harm) or 3 (actual harm) and the scope is widespread.

Impact on Programming

It is generally accepted that providing quality services in activity programming is essential. But there is often great difficulty in defining "quality." Does quality mean that you offer activities seven days a week, five times a day? Or does it mean that all your documentation gets done, even if you have to cancel a few of the less popular activities? Each facility may have its own idea of what a quality program looks like. However, with the federal mandate, it becomes even more urgent that specific criteria for defining quality in activities be developed. It is imperative that these areas of criteria be developed by those who are involved in activity programming directly — as they are the best sources to develop an appropriate and realistic definition of "quality."

There is also a "quality of life" requirement in the OBRA regulations that specifies that a facility will "care for its residents in a manner and in an environment that promotes maintenance or enhancement of each resident's 'quality of life.'"[6] This can be evaluated through the residents' satisfaction with their environment, care received and the amount of control they maintain over their life decisions and belongings.

The areas included within this quality of life standard are *Activities*, *Social Services* and *Environmental* issues. More specific information can be found in the Residents' Bill of Rights and the interpretive guidelines to the OBRA Regulations. Your facility will probably have a set of these regulations in a book called the **State Operations Manual** published by the Department of Health and Human Services. This book contains the entire OBRA law and the interpretive guidelines of each element of that law.

Activities departments have long been recognized as being instrumental in assuring quality of life in long term care. Activities are considered to be a "universal" need for all individuals.

In order to assure quality standards in an ever-changing health care setting, programs and personnel must be developed, tested and validated. In short, "quality assurance" and quality of life requirements may be the perfect means for the activities personnel to increase their professionalism and gain continued recognition as a strong link in the team approach to quality care.

Chapter 3

Developing Quality Assurance Programs

In any quality assurance plan, there are basic steps that need to be followed. All of these will be dealt with in chapters of their own, but a brief description of the five steps can be found in the following table.

Simply put, a good quality assurance plan should answer the questions of what is going to be done, how it will be accomplished, who is going to do it and how the results will be measured and evaluated.[7]

And the objectives of such a program should be to:

- provide the best, reasonable care to each resident.
- commit the time, money and/or other resources necessary to correct identified problems.
- whenever possible, correct problems at their source to avoid a reoccurrence of the problem.

The charts on the next two pages show the steps of a quality assurance program and the chapters in the book where information on each step may be found.

Steps of Quality Assurance Program

Step 1	Chapter 4: *Identifying Issues and Selecting Study Topics*	Obviously it is essential to begin with a determination of what service needs to be improved to provide quality service. This first step has you look closely at the problem to specifically identify what is not right. Unfortunately, many quality assurance programs concern themselves with issues that are not important, or with procedural items that can be easily remedied, rather than those that justify being part of long-range planning.
Step 2a	Chapter 5: *Establishing Indicators*	Identifying elements that can be monitored to measure changes made. The elements or characteristics of the service you select to measure should be a general statement about what the service would look like if there was not a problem.
Step 2b	*Developing Criteria*	Developing criteria for each indicator. Writing a plan that spells out exactly what should be found and ideally in what quantity and in what time frame.
Step 3a	Chapter 6: *Determining Methodology*	Establishing the exact method to be used to collect information: from which sources, by whom, how often, how long and how the results are going to be used.
Step 3b	*Collecting Data*	Implementing the chosen methods of data collection.
Step 4a	Chapter 7: *Understanding the Problem*	Reviewing and assessing collected data to see what, where and how serious the problems are. Deciding which problem areas should be the focus of further study.

Steps of Quality Assurance Program (Continued)

Step 4b	Setting Standards	Standards are set to describe the desired outcomes in a measurable way.
Step 4c	Finding Solutions	Searching for possible ways to reach the standards set.
Step 4d	Writing an Action Plan	The methodology for implementing a change is determined along with decisions about who is to have the responsibility and what the time frames will be.
Step 4e	Implementing the Plan	Putting into action the strategies that have been developed.
Step 5a	Chapter 8: Assessing the Outcomes	Did the plan work? Do the problems still remain? Has there been some improvement? This procedure often entails a repeat of steps 3 and 4: going back and re-collecting the data and then analyzing the results to see if the standards have been reached.
Step 5b	Identifying New Issues or Continuing to Work on the Old	If the problems are not solved, new strategies must be planned. If, however, the process has been successful, a new plan should be developed for the next area of focus. As stated earlier, quality assurance is an ongoing process and does not stop once a particular problem is corrected. It is also necessary to periodically go back and monitor earlier plans and see if the goals are continuing to be met. Two or three past issues may be chosen at random for an on-going audit in addition to the main topic of study. These could be changed periodically on a rotating basis to assure that new problems have not arisen in any of these areas.

All staff are held accountable for the quality of life each resident experiences. You must become the observer, the researcher and the doer. The quality assurance studies that you create and oversee should be looked upon as research in the area of quality of life. The results and process of your work can be used not only to assure quality in your facility, but also as an example to other activity professionals. You can focus on excellence and others will soon follow.

Federal and state regulations are guidelines for *minimal* compliance only. Complying with these regulations can be difficult given the typical staffing ratio. But, upon closer examination, the professional can easily point to areas of the regulations that really don't go far enough. The various professional organizations are beginning to define measurable elements of a good practice. But, since the professionals organizations are not in full agreement and the regulations are inadequate, the activity professional may feel at a loss.

Assessing quality care is even more difficult because of this. In P.W. Shaughnessy's opinion, quality can be evaluated by:

- looking at the environment and capacity of the nursing home,
- seeing if the nature of the planning and procedures followed in prescribing and providing care make sense and
- deciding if the change or lack of change in the resident's health status, morale and life style behaviors was for the better.[8]

But, admittedly, there are many factors that influence the resident, the environment and the responses to care that are beyond the control of staff. In the case of quality assurance programs that are service specific, it is usually impossible to determine which department had the greatest impact on the resident. What, if any, intervention might have directly caused the changes that occurred may never be sorted out. For this reason, the quality assurance process is trans-disciplinary.

Quality Assurance Models

The activity professional has many quality assurance models to choose from. All have three things in common: they help identify and prioritize problems, provide a system to monitor the changes and identify when to stop monitoring. The activity professional's national organization as well as the government may provide different models on how to implement a quality assurance program. When selecting a quality assurance model, look at what the various models have to offer. But remember, quality assurance programs work best when the entire facility is working together. Having all staff use the same quality assurance model helps improve communication and reduce conflict.

Regardless of their source, quality assurance models all focus on the three basic approaches or ways to measure change. They are *structure, process* and *outcome.*

Structure models are concerned generally with the settings in which care is provided and the way that the organization is set up, staff qualifications, available facilities, resources and equipment (e.g., facility has activities personnel staffed seven days a week).

Process techniques look at the way in which care is provided: frequency, methods, staff interventions and behaviors (e.g., residents on bedrest will be visited once a day for reality orientation activities).

Outcome assessments are concerned with the end results: that is, what actually happens to the residents as a result of the care that they received.[9,10] Outcome assessments, while certainly the most difficult to measure, are considered by most authorities to be the most important (e.g., residents' reality orientation scores will not drop more then 5% over six months).

Terminology

Regardless of which model is selected, all have basic things in common. Before looking at the specifics of these techniques, it is necessary to have some familiarity with the terms that are standard in quality assurance programs.

Monitoring means observing and checking the quality and appropriateness of care. It is from this process that trends, patterns and potential problems can be identified and quality assurance priorities set.

- Did each resident receive an activity calendar?
- Were residents allowed to walk to the activity if they were able (instead of being placed in a wheelchair)?
- Did the staff chart in a timely manner?
- Did any resident go three days without any contact from an activity staff?

Indicator is a specific component of care that can be monitored to give an accurate picture of the quality of services being provided. Indicators can be outcomes (actual involvement in activities), attitudes (satisfaction with care), processes (every resident is assessed within seventy two hours of admission) and/or use of resources (use of large print books).

Some examples of indicators which may be used include:

- resident and family satisfaction with the activities program
- little or no change in the level of reality orientation
- little or not loss of range of motion

Criteria are the means by which achievement can be measured. They contain measurable elements that can be used when setting standards.

- Residents (or families) report a given level of satisfaction with the activities program.
- A certain percentage of residents without a diagnosis of dementia retain or improve their scores on reality orientation testing from admission to discharge.
- A certain percentage of residents maintain or improve their range of motion over a period of six months.

Standards refer to desirable and realistic performance expectations for any given department. Their purpose is to measure performance which makes a difference in the actual quality of the care provided. They are commonly developed by professional organizations, regulatory agencies, or other external sources. According to Reynolds and O'Morrow:

> "...it is not so much a question of developing and implementing standards along with having the standards accepted by administrators and accrediting bodies, but more whether the standards assure quality." [11]

The standards must be precise, objective, measurable, realistic, relevant and understandable. Standards for the criteria given above might be:

- At least 85% of the residents will report satisfaction (with a score of 4 = satisfied or 5 = very satisfied) with the activities program.
- At least 95% of all residents without dementia in the sampling group will maintain or improve their reality orientation scores between admission and discharge.
- At least 95% of residents will maintain their range of motion during the next six months. Of those, 50% will experience at least a 10% increase in range of motion of one or more limbs.

Some additional examples of standards include:

- Standard: All residents (100%) will be contacted to see what services or supplies they need at least once every three days over a period of three months.

- Standard: The activity director position will be held by an individual who meets the qualifications outlined in the OBRA regulations.

- Standard: The activity director will implement a program appropriate to the individual needs of the resident including needs related to restoration of function, reduction of a disability and/or rehabilitation to improve the resident's quality of life and maximum level of independence.

Steps in Designing a Quality Assurance Study

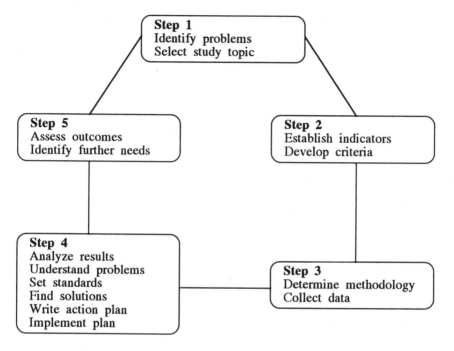

Step 1
Identify problems
Select study topic

Step 5
Assess outcomes
Identify further needs

Step 2
Establish indicators
Develop criteria

Step 4
Analyze results
Understand problems
Set standards
Find solutions
Write action plan
Implement plan

Step 3
Determine methodology
Collect data

Chapter 4

Identifying Issues and Selecting Study Topics

The first step in the quality assurance process is to determine the focus of your program. This can be done in a variety of ways but, most often, the best place to begin is with an informal discussion within the department and with other members of the transdisciplinary team. The task should be to pinpoint the primary functions of the department and those elements or functions that:

- require the most time
- are unique to that specific service
- impact resident care
- involve other departments
- denote "quality"

Methods

From such discussions, it should be possible to identify specific services or job responsibilities that are consistently not getting done on time or to everyone's satisfaction. There are several ways that this may be accomplished:

- Survey residents and their families to provide information on areas that need improvement.
- Review past and present calendars.
- Conduct walk-through observations of activities, individual leisure pursuits and the environment in general.
- Assess the current population and program needs according to functional and cognitive abilities.[12]
- Compare facility procedures or outcomes to recognized standards in the field with the goal of focusing on those areas that aren't up to standards.
- Review recent survey results and plans of correction.

There are several areas that might be looked at for possible quality assurance topics within the activities realm. Very generally, they might include:

- documentation
- the assessment process
- environment
- staff capabilities
- leadership
- policies and procedures
- administrative issues
- community involvement
- resident council
- outings
- infection control issues pertaining to activities
- team approach to restraint reduction
- activity involvement as part of the team assessment
- interventions utilized during group activities
- programming both for groups and one-on-one special needs

You may find that one problem (issue) is that your department needs to have more information about an activity, a service or other job task. Obtaining more information to improve the safety and quality of the work produced is a reasonable quality assurance goal. Examples might be:

- to find out more information about the legal and other aspects of having a pet visitation program
- to find out the needs of residents with diagnoses which are new to your facility (e.g.; AIDS, sub acute care)
- to learn the process required to bill for your services (third party reimbursement)

Government regulations may also be used as a standard to measure your department's performance. It should be kept in mind that regulations are legal requirements and merely making sure that they are being met is not a suitable focus for an on-going study. While regulations usually address only the most minimal standards of care,[13] they could serve as a starting point for improved services.

Common Quality Assurance Issues

Because the job of an activity professional is a dynamic and complex job s/he will find many problems (issues) which could be addressed through a well thought out quality assurance program. The rest of this chapter touches on some of the areas that the activity professional might examine to determine if substandard performance is evident.

Documentation

Documentation is a key part of an activity professional's job and one that is often considered the most tedious and time consuming. Making it part of an ongoing study might help in demonstrating how truly important it is, as well as in making it more efficient and effective.

More often than not, documentation is considered the logical focus of a quality assurance study. However, those elements that are required by regulation (frequency, dates, signatures, timeliness, etc.) are just that — requirements and, as suggested earlier, are not suitable for the subject of a long term study. Despite these exclusions, there are still several possibilities for such as a study under this heading.

Certainly, the content of documentation is something that often can be improved. For example, the content of the initial assessment might be a good topic for study. Does the assessment include:

- a realistic and comprehensive picture of the resident?
- identification of individual interests, needs, previous lifestyle and customary routine?
- a description of behavior and not just labels?
- a listing of assets and strengths?
- specific, measurable and observable goals that refer to a problem or need that was identified in the assessment?
- approaches that are appropriate for the goals set?
- indication that resident's disabilities were considered in the setting of goals and in the selection of activities to implement them?
- the input and involvement of residents and their families in the goal setting and care plan design?

Any or all of these aspects can be used to develop criteria to measure the effectiveness of documentation. (Starting with the next chapter, a documentation example will be used to demonstrate how the process occurs).

As for the Activity Progress Notes, do they reflect:

- changes in attitudes and behaviors (if it occurred)?
- degree and quality of participation?
- progress toward goals?
- attendance patterns?
- indicated changes in goals?
- notes written whenever significant changes take place, not only at required intervals?
- follow-through on implementation of the last care plan?
- responsibilities assigned to the appropriate staff members?
- an activity treatment plan which is part of and keyed into the resident's overall plan of care?

You may want to use the Monitor Sheet for Content of Documentation found in Chapter 6 to determine whether all areas are being addressed in these notes.

Procedures for documentation might also be considered:

- adequacy of forms
- location of copies
- ways in which attendance is kept
- the system by which updates are completed on time

Environment

Another prime concern of activity professionals is the environment in which residents live and staff attempt to provide quality of life and care. As it is their responsibility to provide the most comfortable and stimulating surroundings possible within the institutional setting,[14] numerous possibilities for quality assurance studies become apparent. Environment refers to such elements as:

- opportunities for privacy
- appropriateness and timeliness of decorations
- sensory stimulation aids
- things that enhance the environment
- reality orientation clues and aides
- individual space for display of personal photos and mementos
- resident input and choice of music, television programs and posters in private and public rooms
- staff attitudes
- spaces in the facility that can be used for individual, small and large group activities

Looking specifically at areas where activities are held, there are a number of things that impact their suitability and, thus, the quality of total programming. These include, but certainly are not limited to:

- restrictions on the area's use due to other departments' needs
- proximity of bathrooms
- seating arrangements
- storage
- cleanliness
- safety
- temperature
- noise
- distractions
- interruptions

- lighting
- glare

It would be worthwhile to conduct a study of the facility in an attempt to identify less traditional places for activities that might be more desirable than those currently being used. Accessibility from residents' rooms and the amount of energy required to get there should be additional considerations (i.e. elevators, ramps, long hallways).

Another often overlooked aspect of environmental considerations is the orientation that residents are given to their surroundings. For instance:

- Are all residents taken on tours and shown the various parts of the facility?
- Are they aware of the differences in personnel and their various roles?
- Are there special programs for those who are having difficulties in these areas?

For may residents this is a long term placement and yet they have problems in relating to and functioning within their new "home."

Opportunities for making choices, solving problems and having some measure of control over one's life is also considered part of the environment. Although this is not an exclusive function of the activities department, it certainly qualifies as a prime area for study. "Freedom of Choice" is one of the measures of the federal government's quality of life requirement and, therefore, one that will be closely monitored.

For more information on environment and how to assess this area of quality of life, refer to **Long Term Care** by Best-Martini, Weeks and Wirth.

The forms on the following pages show what OBRA looks at regarding quality of life and the environment. You can use them to check your facility.

OBRA
Quality of Life Review Form

F240 A – Quality of Life
"A facility must care for its residents in a manner and in an environment that promotes maintenance or enhancement of each resident's quality of life."

Requirement	+ = Met — = Not Met Interpretation Date:	
F241 Dignity	Focus on a resident as an individual. Respect for space and property. Treating residents respectfully as adults. Promoting independence and dignity in dining.	
Self Determination and Participation.		
F242 Choose activities, schedules and health care consistent with his or her interests, assessment and plans of care	Accommodating individual schedules and needs according to resident's requests and previous lifestyle and interests.	
F242 Interact with members of the community both inside and outside the facility	Facilitating involvement in community groups and matters which were important to resident before admission.	
F242 Make choices about aspects of his or her life in the facility *that are significant to the resident*	Providing smoking areas to those residents expressing an interest. Therapy schedules are to be worked around activities important to the residents, including his/her favorite television program.	
F243-244 Participation in resident and family groups in the facility	Provide a private space for family and resident groups upon requests.	

OBRA
Quality of Life Review Form, Side 2

Requirement	+ = Met — = Not Met Interpretation	Date:
F243 Facility must provide a designated staff person responsible for providing assistance and responding to written requests that result from group meetings	This staff person listens, records and assists administration with following through with grievances and recommendations.	
F246 Accommodation of Needs (1)..adaptations of the facility's physical environment and staff behaviors to assist residents in maintaining independent functioning, dignity, well-being and self-determination.	Telephone access Personal property Married couples Activities Social Services Psychosocial functioning Homelike environment Activities of Daily Living Accidents and prevention-assertive devices	
F247 (2) ...Receive notice before the residents room or roommate in the facility changes	Accommodation of Needs pertains to how well the team is enhancing and maintaining independence vs. dependence on staff and environment.	

Comments:

36

OBRA
Environment Review Form

F252 Environment
"The facility must provide a safe, clean, comfortable and homelike environment, allowing the resident to use his or her personal belongings to the extent possible."

Be sure to review the *Environmental Assessment Form* to begin problem solving.

\+ = Met

— = Not Met

Requirements	Interpretation	Date:
De-emphasize institutional character	Encourage personal belongings.	
Cleanliness	How clean is the facility? Are there odors detected in any of the rooms and halls?	
Individuality	Do you get to know who this person is and what their past interests were by observing their room and personal things and style?	
Clutter	Are day rooms and private rooms cluttered? Is there space for wheelchair and equipment accessibility?	
F253 Housekeeping and Maintenance services	Assuring cleanliness and infection free environment for resident's equipment and supplies: toothbrush, dentures, denture cups, bed pans, urinals, feeding tubes, leg bags, catheter bags, pads and positioning devices.	

Requirements	Interpretation	Date:
F254 Clean linens that are in good condition	Are there adequate linens available? Are they in good condition and without stains?	
F256 Adequate lighting	Lighting suitable to tasks that residents choose to perform or facility staff must perform? Minimal glare and comfortable to the visually impaired? Is lighting accessible to the resident?	
F257 Comfortable and safe temperature levels	Is the temperature consistently comfortable? Are there any rooms which are noticeably cold or too warm?	
F258 Comfortable sound levels	Is conversation easy or do you have to raise your voice to be heard? Are there many distractions during group events? Are TVs and radios on too loud and too early or late at night?	
F255 Private closet space in each room	Closets must be provided with ample space and accessible shelves for resident use.	

Comments:

OBRA
Activities Potential Review Form

F 272 (x) Activities Potential
"...The resident's ability and desire to take part in activities which maintain or improve physical, mental and psychosocial well-being."

+ = Met

— = Not Met

Requirements	Interpretation	Date:
Residents are offered activities in addition to ADLs.	These would be activity/leisure involvement which a resident pursues for a sense of well being.	
Self-esteem	Focus on the individual. Meaningful activities which highlight the abilities and uniqueness of each resident.	
Health education	Nutrition related activities, wellness, leisure education, relaxation, understanding medical conditions and treatment plans.	
Pleasurable experiences	These can be social activities which encourage passive or active participation. What brings the pleasure is feeling safe, familiar surroundings, rekindling past interests.	
Opportunities for creative expression	Art, creative writing, oral histories, poetry, music, drama, gardening, cooking.	

Requirements	Interpretation	Date:
Opportunities for achieving success	Can be incorporated in all activities at any level. It must be adapted and broken into stages for success at each level.	
Opportunities for achieving financial independence	Money management. Involvement in previous interests such as the stock market, investments and banking.	
Opportunities for achieving emotional independence	Problem solving activities and situations. Creative and expressive outlets. Activities which promote self respect and individuality. Life review. Activities which assist others so that the resident has the chance to continue giving to others.	

Comments:

Another area of environment is the role of activities in the facility. Are the activities a part of daily life (normalization) or just isolated events that occur periodically and are attended by some of the residents? In addition, are there numerous opportunities for residents to be involved in community activities and interests if they choose not to be involved in the facility program?

Staff Capabilities and Leadership

To run a successful program which provides good quality care, each staff person must be properly trained. Every job has its own set of skills and other necessary qualifications. Staff are hired who seem to have all the required skills and qualifications. Frequently though, hiring decisions are based on compromise — a person may be strong in one area that is deemed important but weak in others, or possess certain unique skills, but have little prior experience in working with residents. Even if the staff person fits well into the position, health care is always changing, requiring the activity professional to continually update his/her training. Many facilities find that the quality of the services offered could increase if the staff received additional training.

There is an obvious benefit to services provided if all staff are educated up to the point where they can perform their job efficiently and effectively. Your quality assurance review can be done to determine proficiency in important areas such as:

- effective communication skills with residents, volunteers, families and other staff members
- understanding of the disease process and typical diagnoses
- competency as a group facilitator and leader
- follow-through on tasks

41

- preparation, organization and coordination
- maintenance of working areas and equipment
- knowledge of residents, regulations, safety precautions and the activities offered
- attitudes
- ability to work as a team member
- sensitivity to physical and psychosocial needs of others

One way to evaluate a staff's performance is to develop a checklist of important skills to be demonstrated and tasks to be completed for important aspects of the job. A sample checklist which looks at leadership skills can be found on the next page. This may be filled out by a peer or a supervisor. Another way to evaluate a staff's performance is by developing clearly defined levels of competency (above standards, meets standards, below standards and unacceptable). A sample of this kind of checklist can be found later in this chapter under the section titled *Job Performance.*

Quality Assurance Evaluation of Group Leadership Skills

Directions: The group leader should be observed and evaluated as to his/her general skills in the following areas. (This can also be used as part of a self-evaluation process.) Please note any areas that seem to need improvement and be specific as possible in identifying the particular problems noted. Use the back of the form or additional sheets as needed.

Key: A = Always   M = Most of the time
       S = Some of the time N = Never

Leader's Name:	A	M	S	N
Is prepared for activity?				
Title describes actual program?				
Provides the same activity as posted?				
Has selected appropriate time length?				
Has selected appropriate group size?				
Provides appropriate atmosphere and environment?				
Is prepared with "Plan B"?				
Gives directions clearly?				
Handles group comfortably?				
Deals with problems as they arise?				
Displays knowledge of individual resident goals?				
Makes effort to meet individual interests and needs?				
Meets, greets, seats residents appropriately?				
Encourages group socialization and interaction?				
Meets predetermined purpose of activity?				
Clears work areas/surfaces?				
Utilizes volunteers effectively?				

Specific Comments and Observations:

Volunteer Programs

Although most programs express a need for volunteers, they do not always use them to the greatest advantage. This is often due to the lack of a coordinated and structured plan that spells out how to identify specific needs and recruit accordingly. A quality assurance study might be set up to look at:

- how needs for volunteers are identified and filled
- recruitment, locations and approaches used
- training, orientation, supervision, utilization, recognition and retention methods

Your quality assurance review could ask such questions as:

- Are there enough volunteers?
- Are they doing what really is needed?
- Are they fulfilling their own needs as well as those of the residents?

You may want to use a questionnaire to assess the satisfaction level of your volunteers. A sample questionnaire can be found on the next page.

Evaluation of Volunteer Experience

Name: _____

Job Responsibility: _____

Length of Service: _____

We care a great deal about our volunteers and their opinions. Would you please help us by indicating how you feel about your experience at this facility. Please indicate the extent to which you agree with the following statements by placing the number which best fits your answer on the line in front of each question. Use the key below:

1	2	3	4
Do Not Agree	Disagree Slightly	Agree	Agree Completely

_____ 1. The residents have benefited from my efforts.

_____ 2. I personally have benefited from this experience.

_____ 3. I have been adequately trained for the assignment I am given.

_____ 4. I feel the staff appreciates my efforts and wants me here.

_____ 5. An activities staff person is available when I need help.

_____ 6. Needed equipment and supplies are provided.

_____ 7. I feel staff encourages my suggestions and listens to them.

_____ 8. I have a better understanding of the services provided here.

_____ 9. I have a better understanding of aging and working with those who are older.

Please write in below (and continue on the other side if necessary) any comments or suggestions that you think would benefit future volunteers.

Time Management

Often departments have adequate personnel and volunteers, but do not use them efficiently and effectively. If clear-cut responsibilities are not assigned, overlap and duplication of effort may result and there is the possibility that some things will not get done at all.

How time is spent and what exactly it is spent on are certainly indicators of degrees of quality. It is expected that a certain amount of time is wasted in every job, but it is important to know where that time is going and if some of that waste can be avoided. Each department should know which tasks take priority over others and have a realistic idea of how much time each task takes. Some of the questions that you might want to ask are

- How much of the staff's time is actually spent in resident contact and how much is spent on other things?
- Are these other things really necessary to the job?
- Must they be done by the activities staff themselves?
- Are unique skills, talents and strengths of individual staff members actually being utilized?
- Do opportunities exist for the personnel and the program to grow and avoid stagnation?

As these are just a few of the considerations that impact on the effective use of time and thus, the quality of care, there are many, many more possible methods that can be used. Another way to do a study on time management is to complete a time management calendar for one month and then to review the results. An example of this can be found in the book **Long Term Care.**[15]

Job Performance

Another area to review for possible improvement is the performance of the employees in each department. Employees can do a self-assessment, peer review teams can be set up in which staff members observe and assess each other or supervisors could suggest where individuals might need improvement. If the self-assessment is used, the supervisor should also be willing to take suggestions from other members of the department or from other supervisors. Relationships within the department, time available and/or the seriousness of the deficiencies should all be factors considered to determine the methods used.

One danger is that feelings such as injured pride, resentment and jealousy may result, regardless of which method is used. If this is a problem, then perhaps there are other personnel issues that need to be resolved besides competencies. The department's ability to work well together impacts the quality of resident care and, if problems exist, it is one of the first things to consider in a quality assurance program.

- What are the major problems?
- Are there underlying factors?
- Who else is involved?
- Is there a great deal of emotional interference?
- Can the problems be solved internally or do they require the assistance of an impartial person from outside of the department?
- Is there someone available to fill that bill?
- If not, what other strategies might be tried?

This is certainly not an easy area to tackle, but its impact on the success of any other quality assurance issue makes it essential to attempt. Sometimes just exploring an issue with a problem solving approach can be helpful. It will be openly discussed even if it cannot easily be resolved. At the very least, this may result in some reduction of tension.

Communication of expectations often helps improve the overall quality of services provided. If staff know what meets standards, they are more likely to be able to put their efforts in that direction. A sample job performance statement is included here for you to review. This statement only covers one major job responsibility: to plan and supervise activities for residents and their families. Each position (e.g., activity assistant) may have five or six such statements.

Activity Professional Position

Plan and **Supervise** Activities for Residents and Their Families

Part 1A: Planning and Organizing
Part 1B: Interpersonal Skills
Part 1C: Application of Personal and Technical Knowledge

Major Job Responsibility: Plan and supervise activities for residents and their families. Part 1A.[16]

Performance Criteria	Above Standards	Meets Standards	Below Standards	Unacceptable
Planning and Organizing	Consistently prepares and runs a dynamic and innovative program. Always manages time of self and volunteers. Uniformly works in a neat, efficient and timely manner. Always maintains a safe environment. No supervision needed.	Usually provides a creative program that is able to meet residents' needs and is enjoyable. Effectively manages time of self and volunteers. Usually works in a neat, efficient and timely manner. Usually maintains a safe environment. Little supervision needed.	Often fails to plan activities. Time management of self and volunteers is poor. Often fails to work in a neat, efficient and timely manner. Occasionally maintains an unsafe environment. Frequent supervision is needed.	Activities are haphazard. Misuses time of self and volunteers. Fails to work in a neat, efficient and timely manner. Frequently maintains an unsafe environment. Constant supervision is needed.

Performance Criteria	Above Standards	Meets Standards	Below Standards	Unacceptable
Major Job Responsibility: Plan and Supervise Activities				
Interpersonal Skills	Always facilitates positive interactions. Demonstrates outstanding leadership skills. Anticipates, identifies and resolves interpersonal communication breakdowns before problems surface.	Usually interacts with residents and families in a warm, sincere manner. Usually facilitates positive interactions during activity. Demonstrates good leadership skills. Few valid complaints regarding poor personal communication.	Occasionally fails to facilitate and encourage positive interactions. Demonstrates inadequate leadership skills. Occasionally contributes to interpersonal problems.	Often interacts with others in a negative and non productive manner. Demonstrates little skills as a leader. Often creates interpersonal conflicts due to lack of communication skills.

Performance Criteria	Above Standards	Meets Standards	Below Standards	Unacceptable
Major Job Responsibility: Plan and Supervise Activities				
Application of Personal and Technical Knowledge	Demonstrates extensive knowledge of the aging process, regulations and the disease process as they relate to running activities services.	Demonstrates good working knowledge of the aging process, regulations and the disease process as they relate to running activities services.	Demonstrates poor working knowledge or understanding of the aging process, regulations and the disease process as they relate to running activities services.	Demonstrates little knowledge or understanding of the aging process, regulations and the disease process as they relate to running activities services.

Programming

This should certainly be one of the major target areas of any quality assurance program and here again, the possibilities are endless. Perhaps the most important are

- Is the programming meeting the residents' health care needs?
- Are residents and families satisfied with the program and activities offered?
- How much input do these groups have in determining what those activities will be?
- How much input do other facility staff have in determining what those activities will be?
- How and with what frequency does the activity program touch each resident's life?

Another possible area of exploration is that of *program design and diversity.*

- Are individual, small group and large group activities provided?
- Are suitable activities available for all levels of physical and cognitive functioning?
- Are the safety needs of residents with cognitive impairments being met in large group settings?
- Are activities offered in different locations in the facility for both diversity, accessibility, personal choice and customary routine?
- Are activities designed to meet the creative, physical, spiritual, intellectual, social and orientation needs of the residents?
- Is the current program meeting the needs of the current population both individually and in groups?

51

- Is the program as a whole designed to meet the identified needs and interests of the individual resident?
- Do the activities provide growth for the residents who attend and do they bring them closer to their individual needs and treatment goals?
- Are the activities staff oriented or resident oriented?
- Are activity analyses done for each activity and are the projected goals of the activities being met?
- Are posted activities actually held as advertised?
- Is program scheduling done for the convenience of the staff or the residents?
- Are other things going on in the facility at the same time that may cause conflict for residents?

Other possible issues include:

- continued involvement and contact with the community
- means of transporting residents to activities both in and out of the facility
- involvement of other staff members in assisting at programs
- methods of notifying residents, staff and families of planned activities
- space requirements for conducting activities
- space requirements for the storage of necessary equipment and supplies
- supplies required to provide the types of programs that are indicated by the population

Restraints

The overuse of restraints on residents in long term care settings is a concern in almost every facility. Excessive use of restraints results in reduced range of motion, increased skin break down and an increase in the violation of residents' rights. You may want to review your facility's use of restraints and determine if the increased use of appropriate activities could decrease the restraint use. The entire team needs to assess which residents might be good candidates for a formal restraint reduction program. The decision should be based on an assessment checklist developed by the staff to help identify residents who would benefit from an alternative program (besides restraints). Some quality assurance areas to review in regards to activities and a transdisciplinary approach to restraint reduction could be:

- How effective is the assessment process?
- How does the team review progress and change?
- How does the activity professional determine who might be a good candidate for this program while in activities?
- How can the activity staff assure safety during the group activity?
- How well have the program specifics been communicated, including the expectation for nursing assistants to be involved during the activities?
- Who keeps notes regarding the resident's response to the reduction or alternative during activities?
- Who determines that it is time to re-evaluate the level of need for a specific resident?
- Is the staff following the procedures designated in the policies and procedures for this program?
- How can this study assure quality for future residents in need of this program?

Organization and Administration

This category includes a wide variety of issues that impact the operation of an activities department and, indirectly, the quality of the service from this department. Most of the issues under this heading fall under the "structure" or "process," rather than the "outcome" types of quality assurance audits. Some of these are

- budget
- ordering, inventorying and maintaining supplies
- meeting and committee attendance
- resources
- policies and procedures
- job descriptions
- educational plans
- fund-raising
- public relations

The position of the activities department and its personnel in the facility might also be considered here: are they afforded respect, support and equal status with other departments both on the organizational chart and in actuality?

Selecting a Topic

As you can see, the areas to review are nearly endless. Decide on the area to study by asking what current problem needs immediate attention or what past study needs to be reviewed. Also look at complaints, or issues from the Resident Council meetings or new requirements that the staff have not been trained on yet.

Quality assurance is always a continuous process. So it is possible to start with one topic and when the steps are completed, to choose another and start the cycle again. Or, more ideally, to select around four aspects of care, which, together, indicate a good, balanced program. Use these to evaluate the long term effect on care as changes are made to enhance services.

Whatever approach is used, it is necessary to set priorities by ordering the suggestions and starting with the ones that seem the most critical. When setting priorities there are additional factors that must be considered. For example, before starting such a project, it is important to think about:

- How much time will be spent on it and from where will that time be taken?
- Will this project add to the stress level of already hard-pressed staff?
- What resources need to be committed and what will be the impact on the department?
- What will be the effect on staff morale?
- What kind of stress will the department (and residents) face if this issue is not addressed?

Careful preparation may be needed to avoid individuals seeing the subsequent monitoring as a threat to their job or a criticism of their performance. The goals of the quality assurance program must be fully explained and a commitment to quality care obtained from all staff members. As stated before, each staff member needs to be held accountable for quality of care.

Therefore, it becomes even more critical that issues selected for study be ones that are deemed important, especially the first time around and are issues where substantial improvement can be made and recognized by all concerned.

Whatever means have been used to identify the important issues, the means as well as the results need to be documented. As part of the quality assurance plan, it is important to have a statement of justification — why this particular issue was selected for further study and improvement.

You may want to use a form during your quality assurance meeting to help identify areas that could benefit from a quality assurance review. The next page has a sample form for you to use.

Determination of Possible Quality Assurance Topics

Date of Session: _____
Personnel Attending:

Identification of Primary Department Functions:

Identification of Issue(s) for Study:

Suggested Methods/Indicators/Criteria:

Standards Desired:

Responsible Personnel:

Date for Completion of Initial Study: _____

Date for Follow-Up Meeting: _____

Chapter 5

Establishing Indicators and Developing Criteria

Once you select the *area* to be investigated (e.g., time management, staff performance, resident satisfaction, etc.) and the *issue* in that area that you want to measure, it's time to look at *indicators* and *criteria*. For our example we will use documentation as the area that needs improvement and the content of the documentation as the issue. (Other valid issues in the area of documentation include the timeliness of charting and the usefulness of the attendance sheet.)

Selecting the area to be investigated and the specific aspects to measure are only the beginning steps in this process. The next step is to identify a set of *indicators*. An indicator is something which you can measure. The indicator (or indicators) that can be used to assess effectiveness or quality for each *issue* must be determined.

For each indicator you need to develop the *criteria* that you will use to measure the level of success. Criteria are the measurable elements that you want to watch for improvement. You will want to write your criteria in precise, objective, realistic, relevant and understandable terms.

Establishing *indicators* and developing *criteria* are often done at the same time and by the same methods. In the discussions that result in the identification of the study topics, the means of measuring them frequently become apparent as well. It is the dissatisfaction with current practices that usually leads to a consensus on what the subject of the quality assurance study will be. At the same time you will probably have a good idea what needs to be measured to see a change and the things you want to measure to decide if your care is improving.

To help illustrate, assume that the content of documentation has been selected as the *issue* for a quality assurance study. This may have resulted from the recognition that assessment is not only a primary function of an activity professional's job, but is becoming increasingly vital in measuring the delivery of quality care.

As can be seen on the following page, two *indicators* could then be selected as a determination of adequacy. The first indicator would focus on the initial assessment and nine measurable criteria established. For resident updates eleven criteria would be required. This example is looking at the *process* of documentation. (Process is one of the three models for quality assurance.)

Area: Documentation

Issue: Content of Documentation: Part 1

The meeting of these criteria will be noted on the accompanying monitor sheet. (Shown in Chapter 6.)

Indicator 1: The initial assessment will give an accurate picture of each resident upon admission.

Criteria: The initial assessment will include:

1. a brief description of the resident
2. medical problems
3. physical condition
4. emotional and cognitive state
5. social, leisure, work and religious background
6. previous lifestyle and customary routine
7. perception of problems and placement
8. realistic identification of needs and/or problems
9. meaningful long-term and short-term goals tied to criteria #8

Area: Documentation

Issue: Content of Documentation: Part 2

The meeting of these criteria will be noted on the accompanying monitor sheet. (Shown in Chapter 6.)

Indicator 2: Resident updates will give an accurate picture of residents' progress since the last note was written.

Criteria: The update will include:

1. summary of activities and events attended
2. frequency
3. type of participation
4. socialization
5. encouragement/reassurance needed
6. behaviors and attitudes
7. mental condition, orientation
8. skills demonstrated
9. progress toward goals
10. meaningful long term and short-term goals (new or revised)
11. activity plan outlined (new or revised)

As it is possible to have multiple *criteria* for one *indicator*, it is also possible to have multiple *indicators* for one issue and the same *criteria* for several *indicators*. In the following example, *Resident Satisfaction with Activities Program*, there is a quality assurance issue with two indicators which look at the *outcome* of activities. (Outcome is the second of the three models for quality assurance.)

The next example on *Activity Department Staff Meetings* looks at quality improvement from the perspective of *structure*. (Structure is the third of the three models for quality assurance.)

The process outlined in this chapter is essentially the one that determines how the quality assurance study will proceed. From the type of *indicators* and *criteria* selected, a plan can then be made on the methodology that will be used in the subsequent steps — how data will be collected, what will be monitored and what the *standards* should be.

Area: Programming

Issue: Satisfaction with Activities Program

(The meeting of these criteria will be determined by a resident survey.)

Indicator 1: The majority of residents are satisfied with the activities offered.

Indicator 2: The majority of residents have positive feelings about their relationships with activities personnel.

Criteria: Satisfaction with current program and interactions with personnel will be determined by surveying all capable residents. (Families may respond for residents who are unable to complete surveys.)

Criteria: Satisfaction with a program will be determined by a survey. At the end of all activities on the 15th and 25th of each month, the activity staff will ask the first three people who arrive at each activity if they were satisfied with the scheduled program.

Area: Organization and Administration

Issue: Activity Department Staff Meetings

(The meeting of these criteria will be noted by a check under each category on the monitor sheet found in Chapter 7.)

Indicator 1: Meetings are timely and run efficiently.

    Criteria: Appropriate personnel will attend staff meetings.

    Criteria: Scheduled time and place is convenient for majority of those involved.

    Criteria: Meetings will start and end on time.

    Criteria: An agenda will be set and adhered to.

Chapter 6

Determining Methodology and Collecting Data

As suggested earlier, there are a number of ways that data can be collected. Some of the possibilities include:

- staff meetings
- surveys
- interviews
- observations
- resident council minutes
- comparisons
- chart audits
- utilization reviews

Whatever method or combination of methods is used, the problems chosen for further study must occur frequently enough and be of enough importance to make the effort worthwhile. There must also be some indication that the problems are, indeed, solvable.[17] The idea is to improve care, not to set up time-consuming studies that serve no real purpose. Before collecting data, regardless of the method chosen, it is essential that there be a clear determination of exactly what is being looked for and what needs to be found out. That is, *what would be seen when the problem is solved or the goal is reached.* These considerations determine the method chosen and how it will be implemented — exactly what it is that needs to be measured or monitored.

Monitoring sheets, checklists or surveys are the methodology required for the examples given in the previous chapter.

The Documentation example in the previous chapter has indicators that specify *"The initial assessment will give an accurate picture of each resident upon admission"* and *"Resident updates will give an accurate picture of residents' progress since the last note was written."* In this example, it is obvious that a chart audit would be the appropriate method for collecting the data. The criteria would be listed on a monitor sheet and if they are met, a mark is made under the appropriate column on the sheet. These marks would then be tallied to determine what the percentage of compliance is at the present time. The monitoring sheets on the following pages illustrate how the collected data would be recorded.

Monitor Sheet for Content of Documentation

Directions: After selecting the resident chart to review write the resident's name in the left hand column. The numbers over the remaining column refer to the number indicators (e.g., "1" is the column for *a brief description of the resident*). If the indicated area is present, place a "1" (one) in the column. If the indicated area is not present, place a "0" (zero) in the column. Fill in for each resident in your sample, add columns down, then divide by number of residents to determine the score for each item.

The initial assessment will include:
1. a brief description of the resident
2. medical problems
3. physical condition
4. emotional and cognitive state
5. social, leisure, work and religious background
6. previous lifestyle and customary routine
7. perception of problems and placement
8. realistic identification of needs and/or problems
9. meaningful long-term and short-term goals tied to criteria #8

The update will include:
1. summary of activities and events attended
2. frequency
3. type of participation
4. socialization
5. encouragement/reassurance needed
6. behaviors and attitudes
7. cognitive condition, orientation
8. skills demonstrated
9. progress toward goals
10. meaningful long and short term goals (new or revised)
11. activity plan outlined (new or revised)

Monitor Sheet
Content of Documentation

Indicator 1: The initial assessment will give an accurate picture of each resident upon admission.

Name of Resident	1	2	3	4	5	6	7	8	9	Total

Monitor Sheet

Content of Documentation

Indicator 2: Updates will give an accurate picture of resident's progress since last note.

Name of Resident	1	2	3	4	5	6	7	8	9	10	11	Total

The quality assurance issue of *Resident Satisfaction with the Activities Program* requires a survey of residents and/or families to determine the level of satisfaction with the activities program and personnel. A letter of explanation should accompany the questionnaire that is sent out to families so they will understand the purpose and be more likely to take the time to fill it out. An example of this letter and the survey can be found on the next four pages.

Selecting A Sample

The size of the sample, or the number of residents, charts, activities, etc. to be monitored in collecting data should also be a consideration. Although it may be desirable to assess everyone in a small facility, this may not be possible. In a very large facility 10 to 15% might be a sufficient number, while a larger percentage is required in a smaller facility.

In those instances where sampling is used, it is essential that a representative selection be made. That is, all levels of care, locations, types of residents, lengths of stay, involvement levels and capabilities must be included. This can be done randomly from all that are available, (whether it be chart, resident, family member, activity, etc.) or by selecting, for example, every second, tenth or thirtieth one.

If only a limited number of items are being monitored, all residents should be included and sampling not used at all.[18]

Sample Letter To Accompany Family Questionnaire

Dear Family,

Thank you for entrusting the care of your loved one to us. We hope we are serving him or her — and you — well.

We aim to be the best nursing facility there is, and are continuously trying to improve the quality of care that we provide to our residents.

You can help us to achieve this goal by filling out the short questionnaire that follows this letter. Most of the questions can be answered by simply checking the appropriate box.

Should you like to comment, we have provided space at the bottom of each page. This would be helpful, particularly where you feel that we might improve our service to your family member and you. If you need more space, please continue your comments on other sheets of paper.

You may also want to discuss the issues covered in this questionnaire with your family member in order to provide as complete and accurate a picture as possible.

In addition, if you have any questions that you would like me to answer, there is space for your name and telephone number at the end to the questionnaire. Otherwise, it is not necessary to identify yourself.

After you have finished, kindly enclose the questionnaire in the stamped, self-addressed envelope that has been provided.

I look forward to receiving this questionnaire from you. Thank you for your help.

Sincerely,
(Administrator)

Family Questionnaire

Most of the items below require only a check mark in the appropriate box based on a scale of "1" to "5" using the key below. In addition, at the bottom of each page, you may want to comment on these items, particularly where there are problems or outstanding performance.

5	4	3	2	1
Excellent	Good	Fair	Poor	No Opinion

Overall

5 4 3 2 1 **Please rate:**

☐☐☐☐☐ Considering everything — services, staff, living conditions, etc., — how would you rate our facility on how well it is serving your family member?

On Admission **Please rate:**

☐☐☐☐☐ The information you got about our center and its programs prior to or upon admission of your family member.

☐☐☐☐☐ The extent to which staff members obtained background information and advice on the best way to care for your family member.

On Care **Please rate:**

☐☐☐☐☐ How well physicians' orders are followed in caring for your family member.

☐☐☐☐☐ Your family member's appearance in terms of cleanliness and being well-groomed.

☐☐☐☐☐ The therapy programs your family member receives.

☐☐☐☐☐ The extent to which help is given to your family member when he or she needs it.

Comments:

On Staff and Facility Interaction

5	4	3	2	1	Please rate:
					Respect and kindness shown your family members by the staff.
					Care taken to protect your family member's privacy.
					Encouragement given your family member to make full use of the center and its programs.
					Extent to which your family member feels comfortable with the staff at the center.
					Extent to which *you* feel welcome when visiting your family member.
					Your ability to communicate (phone, mail, visit) with your family member without limitations set by the center.
					Accessibility of staff by phone or in person to meet with you and address your concerns about your family member.
					Extent to which the staff keeps you informed about your family member.

On Environment

					Please rate:
					The center as a whole on cleanliness, comfort, home-like atmosphere and being odor-free.
					The opportunities that exist for your family member to individualize and have some personal belongings in his or her own room.
					Extent to which your family member's belongings are respected and kept in an attractive, orderly manner.

Comments:

On Activities

5   4   3   2   1   **Please rate:**

Extent to which a variety of activities are offered to your family member.

Extent to which your family member is consulted as to what he or she would enjoy doing.

Relationship of your family member's past interests to his or her present activities.

Degree to which your family member's past preferences are considered in terms of scheduling location, duration, etc.

The number and variety of social opportunities that are available for your family member.

Degree of satisfaction that your family member expresses in the activities that he or she attends.

On Food Service   **Please rate:**

Extent to which food served is to your family member's specific likes and dislikes.

Atmosphere in the dining rooms — whether it is pleasant and well-maintained.

Assistance given during meals, if needed.

Comments:

76

Chapter 7

Taking Action

Having collected the necessary data and information, the next step is to work out a solution to the problem being studied. Identifying the problems is the half way point of any quality assurance project. Setting up a plan for resolution should be the main goal of the whole process. Unfortunately, this is often the weakest part of the whole procedure and as Kane and Kane point out, "many more problems are identified than corrected."[19]

The data collected must be analyzed and a determination made to decide:

1. What problems need to be addressed?
2. What should be the ideal goals or standards?
3. What actions need to be taken to achieve them?

Understanding the Problem

Too often, the problem itself is not clearly understood, so the solution is difficult to identify. Many times what seems to be the problem on the surface is the result of underlying factors. Possible causes need to be identified — is the problem due to:

- lack of knowledge, aptitude, or skill on the part of the staff?
- faulty facility policies and procedures?
- organizational or environmental barriers?

It has been suggested in the "Quest for Quality" program that after each assessment, four basic questions need to be asked:

- "What problems have been identified?"
- "What are possible causes?"
- "What is an appropriate goal that will indicate reduction or elimination of the problems?"
- "What plan of action will accomplish this goal?"[20]

Setting Standards

A *standard* is a measurable description of how something should be done. Standards are the expected performance for any function or component of care provided by the department. You have already determined the problem (indicator) and the ways you are looking at the current situation (criteria). Now write out realistic, measurable, and observable descriptions (standards) so you can really tell that the problem is taken care of. Standards involve the setting of goals to be achieved. How do you determine what the standard should be? Standards can be selected from a review of current professional literature, practice and/or a determination of what is possible in the given setting.

The data collected should be examined to pinpoint differences between these expected or desired results (standards) and the current situation.[21] Whenever possible, the results should be stated in measurable, numerical terms such as percentages, to make knowing when you reached the standard a much easier task. But again, it is essential to identify what the goal of the standards should be.

Referring back once again to the documentation example, standards might be stated as:

For Indicator 1: *Initial assessments will include all nine of these factors 100% of the time.*

For Indicator 2: *Resident updates will include all eleven of these factors 100% of the time.*

Given the nature of the *criteria*, it is not unreasonable or unrealistic to expect that the necessary information will be included 100% of the time, although this may not happen right away. Of course, the length of time required to achieve the standard would depend on the current rate of compliance and, as will be pointed out in the next section, what the problems that account for the current rate of compliance are.

Standards for the other two examples are shown on the next two pages.

Area: Programming

Issue: Satisfaction with Activities Program

(Meeting the criteria will be determined by resident surveys.)

Indicator 1: The majority of residents are satisfied with the activities offered.

Indicator 2: The majority of residents have positive feelings about their relationships with activities personnel.

Criteria: Satisfaction with current program and interactions with personnel will be determined by surveying all capable residents. (Families may respond for residents who are unable to complete surveys.)

Standard: At least 80% of those completing surveys express satisfaction with current program.

Standard: At least 80% of those completing surveys express positive feelings about relationships with activities personnel.

Criteria: Satisfaction with a program will be determined by a survey. At the end of all activities on the 15th and 25th of each month, the activity staff will ask the first three people who arrive at each activity if they were satisfied with the scheduled program.

Standard: At least 80% of the residents surveyed will indicate satisfaction with the program.

Area: Organization and Administration

Issue: Activity Department Staff Meetings

(Meeting these criteria will be noted by a check under each category on the accompanying monitor sheet.)

Indicator 1: Meetings are timely and run efficiently.

Criteria: Appropriate personnel will attend staff meetings.

Criteria: Scheduled time and place is convenient for majority of those involved.

Criteria: Meetings will start and end on time.

Criteria: An agenda will be set and adhered to.

Standard: All of these conditions will be met at least 75% of the time.

Monitor Sheet
Activity Department Staff Meetings

+ = Criteria Met
— = Criteria Not Met

Meeting Dates

Criteria									
Appropriate staff attend meeting (% of staff attending). *90% or greater = met*									
Schedule time/place does not conflict with days off or resident care planning meetings. *90% or greater = met*									
Start and end as scheduled. Starts, ends within 5 minutes of scheduled time. *100% = met*									
Agenda posted before meeting — followed. *100% = met*									
Total									
Standard	%	%	%	%	%	%	%	%	%
75% (3 out of 4) of the above listed criteria are met each staff meeting. *+ = met — = not met*									

Finding Possible Solutions

A number of options are possible to address the question of why there is a problem. Policies, attitudes, resources, knowledge or skills may be identified as the things that need to be changed.[22] What appears to be the best possible approach or combination of approaches should be selected, keeping in mind the particular needs of your department and organization. And then, of course, the change must be implemented.

Some of the possible methods or resources for corrective action include:

- journals or reference books that address identified problems
- inservice education
- continuing education programs
- practice in deficient areas
- counseling
- consultants
- implementation of time management techniques
- improved communication with other departments
- redistribution of staff
- revision of policies and procedures
- pairing of staff (peer training)
- group or team meetings
- additional staff and/or volunteers
- introduction of new activities
- re-structuring of present activities
- revisions in calendars
- providing activities in new locations

- increased community involvement
- improved volunteer recruitment, orientation, supervision, and/or retention
- increased resources
- environmental modifications

One or more of the first fourteen methods listed might be considered as a means of reaching the standards in the documentation example being used.

Completing a written analysis of activities to identify the activity's physical, cognitive and social requirements may also help in the solution of problems that have to do with meeting individual residents' identified needs and interests.

Writing Action Plans

An action plan is a statement (or statements) which say what actions the staff will take to correct the problem. Plans for remedial action should include:

- who or what is expected to change
- the person responsible for implementing the change
- the actions to be taken to effect this change
- when the actions should occur

You will want to keep a written record of the actions that you have taken or plan to take. The next two pages have forms which may be used to keep a record of your written quality assurance plan of action.

Quality Assurance Follow-Up Plan

Topic Chosen for Study: _____

Date: _____

Statement of Justification/Reason for Choosing this Topic:
(This statement should reflect results of monitoring activities.)

Standards Desired:

Deviation from Standard Identified:

Selected Method and Plan for Improvement:

Date for Completion: _____
Responsible Person: _____
Date for Completion of Follow-Up study: _____

Activity Quality Assurance and Continuing Quality Improvement Form

Area to Be Reviewed	Study Plan and Anticipated Outcome	Review Dates

Re-evaluation Notes:

1st Month

2nd Month

3rd Month

Completed by: _____ Date: _____ Quarterly Review: (QA Committee) _____ Date: _____

Implementing the Plan

Once you have your basic quality assurance plan written, you will need to consider the length of time it is likely to take to make a change. Allocating enough time for the change to occur should always be part of the plan and actions should address the cause, scope and severity of the problem.

One of the issues that often needs to be addressed in designing quality assurance studies is the amount of time and effort used and the paperwork that is generated by these activities. Staff often complain that this is just one more thing that takes them away from their "real job" — time spent with residents. Although initial studies do take a lot of time and resources, they eventually become part of the routine and are far less time-consuming.

Additional benefits often are derived from *improved morale, increased competencies* and *better resident care.* Costs should be weighed against these benefits to see if the quality assurance plan is really effective. And most importantly, a topic should be chosen that is sufficiently significant and has enough impact to justify this use of resources.[23]

Chapter 8

Assessing Outcomes and Identifying New Issues

Having a quality assurance program which you check regularly is now considered to be as much a part of your job as resident assessment and running activities. Because your participation in a quality assurance program will take time, you will want to check every now and then to make sure that the program is working for you, not the other way around. The on-going appraisal of the quality assurance program should be designed to evaluate:

- How is it impacting or improving the resident care?
- How well are the identified problems being resolved?
- How effective is the monitoring methodology?

The purpose of any quality assurance study is to ensure the provision of care that meets the needs of the population served. And it is that population who should be surveyed to determine if, indeed, they are satisfied with the results. "Consumer satisfaction," the focusing on what the consumer considers to be important outcomes, should be the measurement of success.[24]

While you are learning to be comfortable with the process of implementing a quality assurance program, outcomes should always be the focus, not the methodology. It is necessary to realize that while plans may have been implemented correctly, the actual problem may not have been correctly assessed. Or, the plan may have fallen short of addressing the actual changes needed.

If problems have been resolved, care improved and resident needs satisfied, then the quality assurance program can be judge successful. To ensure that the change made continues to provide improved quality, data should be taken periodically.

If only some improvement is noted, then a determination must be made as to whether sufficient time was allotted, alternate measures are required (changes to the action plan), or if this is the maximum improvement possible (resetting the standards).

When the problem being studied is solved to the extent that your standards are met, the process should begin again with a new problem or area that needs improvement.

You need to look upon quality assurance as a continuous process that is as much a responsibility for activity professionals as any other function that they do. By making quality assurance a regular part of your work you will increase the excellence of the services that you provide and will be able to demonstrate the impact these activities have on improving the "quality of life."

Chapter 9

Getting Ready for Survey

The activity professional is responsible for the constant review of his/her program and standards with a priority issue being addressed at least quarterly. In reviewing a program, the department head needs to know:

- the applicable federal and state regulations
- how close the department is to being in "substantial compliance"
- where the problems and issues lie and how to address them
- what the department is going to do to solve a problem or to strengthen a weak area
- how the activity professional will monitor and evaluate progress
- what tools will be needed

During the survey process, the Survey Team may wish to see information relating to the Quality Assurance Program. By law, they are allowed to review the policy and procedures related to QA, but the specific documentation of the current quality assurance study and past studies do not need to be brought forth for review as this is an internal monitoring process. You may refer to Tag 521 at the end of this chapter for clarification.

Thus, each department's Quality Assurance plan should be designed to:

- determine that their services are needed (In the case of Long Term Care, activities is a required service.)
- justify the resources and personnel used
- measure their impact upon those served
- serve as a problem solving tool
- raise staff consciousness and commitment to quality
- assure continued compliance with federal and state regulations

Policies and Procedures

Each department is expected to have written directions which explain how staff are to carry out the various parts of their jobs. The department needs to have a set of policies and procedures which outline how the quality assurance program will be run. In addition, there will be quite a few policies and procedures which explain to staff how to carry out a task while still meeting standards.

A *policy* is a decision made by management which states what should be done. The *procedure* which follows the management statement lists the steps that need to be taken to fulfill the intent of the management statement. This list (procedure) clearly outlines:

- who is to do what,
- when they are to do it and
- how they are to do it.

There are two policies and procedures included in this chapter for you to review. If you would like further help in writing policies and procedures you may want to read **How to Write Policies, Procedures and Task Outlines** by Larry Peabody (1995) and **The Album of Activity Policies and Procedures** by Beth Hall, Carole Hotelling and Michele Nolta (1995). Both are available through Idyll Arbor, Inc.

Activities Quality Assurance Policy and Procedure

Policy:
It is the policy of this facility to have a quality assurance program in place for self-monitoring and evaluation.

Procedures:
The Activity Professional will:
1. Be an active member of the QA Committee as an transdisciplinary team member.
2. Identify an area of priority focus for the activities department.
3. Follow the facility policies and procedures as they relate to the quality assurance program.
4. Gather input from other team members as to the validity of the study as well as the findings of the study if it is an activity issue.
5. Utilize appropriate forms to document the QA process.
6. Complete all forms relating to the QA process.
   Some of these forms may be:
   - Needs Assessment Form
   - Activity Quality Assurance and CQI Form
   - Environmental and Activity OBRA Review Forms
7. Review all QA studies on a quarterly basis as a QA committee member.
8. Continue to use the CQI as a means of following through and complying with previous studies.

Accepted: _____
Reviewed: _____
Revised: _____

Individual and Room Bound Activities (Room Visits)[25]

Policy:
It is the policy of this facility to provide adequate activity contacts and/or opportunities to those residents who are unable to leave, or who choose to stay primarily in their own rooms. The activities shall be reflective of each resident's individual activity interests. The full realm of activity programs that are offered to residents in group settings, are offered with adaptations and modification to residents who are room bound and/or bed bound, or prefer to remain primarily in their rooms.

Procedures:
The activity staff will ...

- Maintain communication with the Nursing Department, to keep apprised of residents who are physically unable to leave their rooms to attend activity programs.

- Maintain a record of residents who choose not to leave their room to attend activity programs, and residents who have patterns of low participation or attendance in group activity programs.

- Provide one-on-one based activity programs to the above stated residents. The in-room activity programs will directly reflect the resident's assessed individualized activity interests.

- Train and coordinate support staff and train volunteers to provide some of the in-room activities to the residents.

- Provide activity contacts according to each resident's requests, needs and interests. The room visits may include, but need not be limited to books, musical tapes, stimulation of the five senses (touch, taste, smell, hearing and sight), reality awareness, craft projects, manicures and simple exercise.

- Engage resident to his/her capabilities within each activity visit to promote and provide social, cognitive, physical and emotional well-being, to stimulate or provide solace, to promote self-respect, self-expression, personal responsibility and choice. Use the activity care plan as a guide to each resident's activity care needs.

- Store materials for the above stated activity in portable boxes, baskets or carts.

- Maintain a record of residents receiving room visits in the activity office.

- Record the specific contents of the room visits on each resident's activity attendance sheet. Complete documentation to record visits: date, activity provided, resident's responses and brief comments as pertinent. Include a summary of this information in the resident progress records as an alternative or addition to the above.

Accepted: _____
Reviewed: _____
Revised: _____

OBRA Quality Assurance Regulations

The **State Operations Manual** provides you with the specific wording of the regulations and with the official interpretation of each regulation. The information on quality assurance below is directly from the **State Operations Manual** (June 1995).

Quality Assessment and Assurance

Guidance to Surveyors — Long Term Care Facilities[26]

Tag 520: (1) A facility must maintain a quality assessment and assurance committee consisting of — (i) the director of nursing services; (ii) a physician designated by the facility; and (iii) at least three other members of the facility's staff. (2) The quality assessment and assurance committee —
Tag 521: (i) meets at least quarterly to identify issues with respect to which quality assessment and assurance activities are necessary; and (ii) develops and implements appropriate plans of action to correct identified quality deficiencies. (3) A State or Secretary [an official in the health care administration] may not require disclosure of the records of such committee except insofar as such disclosure is related to the compliance of such committee with the requirements of this section. (4) Good faith attempts by the committee to identify and correct quality deficiencies will not be used as a basis for sanctions.

Intent: 483.75(o) The intent of this regulation is to ensure the facility has an established quality assurance committee in the facility which identifies and addresses quality issues and implements corrective action plans as necessary.

Guidelines: 483.75(o) The quality assessment and assurance committee is responsible for identifying issues that necessitate action of the committee, such as issues which negatively affect quality of care and services provided to residents. In addition, the committee develops and implements plans of action to correct identified quality deficiencies. The medical director may be the designated physician who serves on this committee pursuant to 483.(o)(1)(ii).

Procedures: 483.75(o) This requirement is reviewed only after completion of Phase 2 sampling. There are two phases to the quality assurance review. During Phase 1 for all facilities:

- The survey team should review how the quality assurance committee functions. Determine through interviews with administrative staff and Quality Assessment and Assurance Committee members if the facility has a Quality Assurance Committee which meets the requirements in 483.75(o).
- Determine if the committee has a formal method to identify issues in the facility which require quality assessment and assurance activities. The facility should also have a method to respond to identified issues and a means to evaluate the response to these issues.

Phase 2 of the review should be conducted if the survey team has identified quality issues. During Phase 2:

- Verify, through interviews with committee members and, as necessary, direct care staff that the committee has established a protocol or method for addressing specific quality problems in the facility that the facility believes have now been resolved.

- Do not review committee records identifying details of the specific quality deficiencies. Surveyors should not focus on if the quality assurance committee has identified and addressed deficiencies which the survey team identifies. Concentrate on verifying that the facility has a quality assurance committee which addresses quality concerns and that staff know how to access that process.

Probes: 483.75(o) When conducting interviews:
- How are facility policies and clinical policies reviewed based on quality assurance findings?

Chapter 10

Joint Commission on Accreditation of HealthCare Organizations

Up to now much of the information you have read dealt with quality assurance in general and government (OBRA) requirements specifically. In all health care settings there is some system of review. This review or survey may occur for licensure or it may be to see if a facility meets all of the federal, state, and county regulations and/or corporate guidelines.

For many long term care settings, the most familiar review is the annual state survey. Each facility is held accountable to the standards addressed in both the state and the federal regulations. It is important to remember that these are minimum standards, and that any professional organization or agency should aspire to a greater standard above and beyond the minimum — especially in these ever changing and competitive times in the health care arena.

Some facilities voluntarily decide to participate in an additional set of rules and standards. The most commonly selected additional set of standards are those of the Joint Commission on Accreditation of HealthCare Organizations.

The Joint Commission on the Accreditation of HealthCare Organizations (JCAHO) was designed to set this higher level of accountability and quality in health care settings. A health care agency will contact the Joint Commission and request an accreditation survey. This survey is scheduled for a specific time period and a cost for this service is charged to the agency. Long term care settings are offering a greater diversity of care, and the consumer is expecting the highest-quality care for their money, so more and more settings are requesting JCAHO Accreditation. You may find yourself working for an agency beginning this process or renewing their accreditation through future surveys. This chapter will give you a brief overview of JCAHO, its history and mission statement and information pertaining to its survey process.

Joint Commission's Mission

The Joint Commission on Accreditation of HealthCare Organizations is dedicated to improving the quality of care that the consumer receives. The Joint Commission is organized as a not-for-profit organization which functions independently of the government, professional organizations (such as the American Hospital Association) and other special interest groups (such as the American Association of Retired Persons). While the Joint Commission is independent of the government, it does contract with the government to provide specific services including surveys.

The Joint Commission's mission is to provide services which encourage health care organizations such as hospitals and nursing homes to continually increase the quality of services they provide to consumers. The Joint Commission does this in part, through the issuance of health care standards and by running a voluntary survey program. When a health care organization passes a Joint Commission survey it is then "Accredited" as having met *professional standards*. These professional standards are meant to reflect what professional groups consider to be good care, not the minimum standards which are reflected in the OBRA survey.

History

Founded in 1951, its members include the American College of Physicians, the American College of Surgeons, the American Dental Association and the American Medical Association. The major functions of the Joint Commission include "developing accreditation standards, awarding accreditation decisions and providing education and consultation to health care organizations."[27]

The Joint Commission offers many different kinds of accreditation, each with its own set of standards. In addition to the accreditation for long term care, including subacute programs and dementia special care units other accreditation programs include:[28]

- hospitals
- nonhospital-based psychiatric and substance abuse organizations, including community mental health centers, freestanding chemical dependency providers and organizations that serve people with mental retardation or other developmental disabilities
- home care organizations
- ambulatory care organizations
- pathology and clinical laboratory services
- health care networks

Not until the late 1960's did the Joint Commission formally become involved in long term care. In 1966, the Commission received a request for accreditation from the American Association of Homes for the Aged and the American Nursing Home Association (now known as American Health Care Association). With data based on research of future trends in the industry from the JCAHO Change Initiative Committee, the first Long Term Care Standards Manual was published in 1990.

The Joint Commission has historically chosen to go its own way when it comes to terminology and certain aspects of the survey process. The government calls the process of assessing, modifying and monitoring the quality of services *Quality Assurance* or QA. The Joint Commission calls this process (as of 1996) *Improving Organizational Performance* or IOP. While the government has remained fairly consistent in its terminology over the years, the Joint Commission tends to change the terms it uses every few years. The Joint Commission does not necessarily make its specific survey findings available to the public while the government requires that the facility have a copy of the full OBRA survey document available upon demand from anyone who asks. The government conducts surveys every year, the Joint Commission every three years. It is important for the activity professional to understand differences to do well on both surveys.

In November 1995, the newest **Comprehensive Accreditation Manual for Long Term Care and Survey Process** was published. (It has a 1996 copyright.) The standards manual includes descriptions of the rationale and meanings of each section. This manual contains both the *standards* for long term care and the *intent statements* for Sub Acute Units and

Dementia Special Care Units. If the setting includes either a sub-acute unit or special care unit, the staff are responsible for adhering to the over-all standards and structuring their services to also match the intent statements geared toward those units.

The standards in the Joint Commission's manuals are all performance based, or "outcome objectives." Along with the standards, the manual provides scoring tools which are very user-friendly.

Categories of Accreditation

When surveying one of these settings, the JCAHO survey team must agree upon the specific level of accreditation the facility is to receive. These levels, or categories are

- Accreditation with Commendations,
- Accreditation,
- Conditional Accreditation,
- Provisional Accreditation or
- Not Accredited.[29]

When accredited, this award is valid for a three year period. If an organization receives *conditional accreditation, no accreditation* or the surveyor finds a serious situation with the potential for jeopardy to resident or public health, the Joint Commission provides information directly to the federal, state or local agency responsible for compliance.

Terminology

Following are some terms commonly used in JCAHO language.

Accreditation: A determination by the Joint Commission that an eligible organization has met standards which apply to that type of health care organization.

Compliance: The ability of a facility to demonstrate that it has met standards and other requirements outlined in the Joint Commission standards manual. Also called "compliance with a standard."

Criteria: Statements about expected performance which can be used to measure how close the actual performance came to meeting expectations.

Data: Uninterpreted material, facts or clinical observations collected as part of the assessment process.

Focused Survey: An in-depth review of one or more aspects of care provided by the health care organization. This type of survey is usually used by the Joint Commission as a check back survey to review how well the health care organization was able to fix a previously identified problem area.

Health Care Organizations: A generic term used to describe organizations that provide health care services.

Intent of Standard: A brief explanation of a standard's rationale, meaning and significance.

Performance Measure: A means of gauging how well the facility executed the tasks necessary to provide quality care.

Performance measures are usually written as standards or indicators.

The activity professional who works in a facility which complies with OBRA regulations and voluntarily goes for Joint Commission accreditation will need to be familiar with two sets of standards and terms. The overall reasons for and processes of quality assurance do not change between the two types of survey. However, the activity professional will need to read two different standards manuals (OBRA and the **Comprehensive Accreditation Manual for Long Term Care and Survey Process**) and be able to use terminology from both.

Footnotes

[1]Ostrow, P., Williamson, J. and B. Joe. 1983. **Quality Assurance Primer**. Rockville, MD: American Occupational Therapy Association.

[2]Herbelin, K. 1988. "Components of a Quality Assessment and Assurance Program." *Contemporary LTC*, May, 70-71.

[3]**State Operations Manual**, Nursing Home Survey Protocol and Enforcement Regulation Training Manual. June, 1995. Department of Health and Human Services. Baltimore: MD

[4]Overheads and Resource Information, Final Rule Training by CARF, *QCHF, CAHSA, CAHHS, June, 1995 (pg. 65)*.

[5]American Health Care Association. *Provider Magazine*, May 1995. pages 10-11.

[6]OBRA regulations list "Quality of Life" as one of the conditions of participation in the Medicare program.

[7]Moeller, D. 1981. "What's So Different about Quality Assurance in Small, Rural Hospitals?" *Hospitals*, 55(11), 7-82.

[8]Shaughnessy, P.W. 1989. "Quality of Nursing Home Care." *Generations*, XIII (1), 17-20.

[9]Nordstrom, M. J. 1980. "Criteria Leading to Quality Controlling Rehabilitation: The Elderly Patient — A Team Member." *Journal of Gerontological Nursing*, 6(8), 457-462.

[10]Applebaum, R. 1989. "What's All This About Quality?" *Generations* XIII (1), 5-7.

[11]Reynolds, R. & O'Morrow, G. (1985) **Problems, Issues and Concepts in Therapeutic Recreation**. Englewood Cliffs, NJ: Prentice Hall, Inc. page 104.

[12]See *Needs Assessment Form and Guidelines for Use* on page 114 of **Long Term Care**, 1994, Best Martini, Weeks, and Wirth. Ravensdale, WA: Idyll Arbor, Inc.

[13]Donovan, G. 1987. "You Want Me to Do What? Regulatory Standards in Therapeutic Recreation" in B. Riley (Ed.) **Evaluation of Therapeutic Recreation Through Quality Assurance**. State College, PA: Venture Publishing, Inc.

[14]Cunninghis, R. 1989. "The Purpose and Meaning of Activities" in Deichman and Kociecki (Eds.), **Working with the Elderly: An Introduction**. Buffalo, NY: Prometheus Books.

[15]The book **Long Term Care** (1994) by Best Martini, Weeks and Wirth has an example of a time management calendar. Ravensdale, WA: Idyll Arbor, Inc.

[16]Modified from job performance criteria, Children's Hospital and Medical Center, Seattle, WA.

[17]Ostrow, P., J. Williamson and B. Joe, 1983. **Quality Assurance Primer.** Rockville, MD: American Occupational Therapy Association.

[18]American Health Care Association. 1982. **Quest for Quality.** Washington DC: AHCA.

[19]Kane, R. A. and R. L. Kane. 1989. "Reflections on Quality Control." *Generations,* XIII (1), 63-68.

[20]Trocchio, J. and J. Holloway. 1990. "Quest for Quality" *Geriatric Nursing.* January/February, 34-36.

[21]Wright, S. 1987. "Quality Assessment: Practical Approaches in Therapeutic Recreation." In B. Riley (Ed.), **Evaluation of Therapeutic Recreation Through Quality Assurance.** State College, PA: Venture Publishing, Inc.

[22]Ostrow, P., J. Williamson and B. Joe. 1983. **Quality Assurance Primer.** Rockville, MD: American Occupational Therapy Association.

[23]Ostrow, P., J. Williamson and B. Joe. 1983. **Quality Assurance Primer.** Rockville, MD: American Occupational Therapy Association.

[24]Kane, R. A. and R. L. Kane. 1989. "Reflections on Quality Control." *Generations,* XIII (1), 63-68.

[25]Used with permission from **The Album of Activity Policies and Procedures** by Hall, Hotelling and Nolta. 1995. San Diego, CA.: Recreational Therapy Consultants.

[26]**State Operations Manual,** DHHS, June 1995, page PP-201, revision 274. Baltimore: MD.

[27]JCAHO 1996 **Comprehensive Accreditation Manual for Long Term Care,** pg. 686. Chicago, IL: JCAHO.

[28]JCAHO 1996 **Comprehensive Accreditation Manual for Long Term Care,** pg. 5. Chicago, IL: JCAHO.

[29]JCAHO 1996 **Comprehensive Accreditation Manual for Long Term Care,** pg. 12-13. Chicago, IL: JCAHO.